52 Question on the Nationalization of Canadian Railways

J.M. Dent & Sons

Copyright © BiblioLife, LLC

BiblioLife Reproduction Series: Our goal at BiblioLife is to help readers, educators and researchers by bringing back in print hard-to-find original publications at a reasonable price and, at the same time, preserve the legacy of literary history. The following book represents an authentic reproduction of the text as printed by the original publisher and may contain prior copyright references. While we have attempted to accurately maintain the integrity of the original work(s), from time to time there are problems with the original book scan that may result in minor errors in the reproduction, including imperfections such as missing and blurred pages, poor pictures, markings and other reproduction issues beyond our control. Because this work is culturally important, we have made it available as a part of our commitment to protecting, preserving and promoting the world's literature.

All of our books are in the "public domain" and some are derived from Open Source projects dedicated to digitizing historic literature. We believe that when we undertake the difficult task of re-creating them as attractive, readable and affordable books, we further the mutual goal of sharing these works with a larger audience. A portion of BiblioLife profits go back to Open Source projects in the form of a donation to the groups that do this important work around the world. If you would like to make a donation to these worthy Open Source projects, or would just like to get more information about these important initiatives, please visit www.bibliolife.com/opensource.

52 QUESTIONS
ON THE
NATIONALIZATION
OF
CANADIAN RAILWAYS

BY
FABIUS

J. M. DENT & SONS, LTD.
MELINDA STREET, TORONTO

Copyright, Canada, 1913
By J. M. Dent & Sons, Limited
Toronto

IN THE FIRST PLACE

CONCEALED in a comparatively innocent matter lie two others of great importance. Nominally, it is the Canadian railway question: actually it is a question of Canadian prosperity, and, ultimately, a question of which political system we believe in—Bureaucracy, to fight which we have spent money and Canadian lives—or Democracy. The Canadian railway question pierces to the quick of all Anglo-Saxon political thinking, challenging an ideal for which our kind have struggled for centuries, an ideal for which Canadian lives have been sacrificed without stint—Democracy!

I believe in Socialism but not Prussian Socialism or Bureaucratic Socialism whose purpose is not the raising and strengthening of the

"52 QUESTIONS"

Individual within the Brotherhood called the State, but the raising and strengthening of the State above and upon the Individual. Let us have none of it.

IT is only prudent to be slow to act in-this matter of Railway Nationalization. Nothing can be lost by delay—the roads are better operated to-day than in the United States. Everything may be gained —including the experience of the British and American Governments who have been less fortunate with their railways than we have been and who will decide in the next two or three years whether or not to purchase their railways as we are asked now to purchase ours. Let us at least not cruise ahead of them in such dangerous seas.

I

Who Loses by Railway Nationalization?

THE railway shareholders? No! They will be allowed to lose nothing. Shares will be purchased or expropriated and they are almost certain to command a better price from the Canadian Government than in the open market. For no nation, if I judge rightly, will knowingly offend the men and women whose money constitutes one of the three essentials of Production: Capital.

These people, receiving back their Capital undiminished, will reinvest it in other businesses just as vital to our affairs as railways, and probably more profitable. I say more profitable because I observe that the

"52 QUESTIONS"

rates and the quality of Canadian railway service are regulated by the Dominion Board of Railway Commissioners, a court responsible to Parliament, while on the other hand many large and essential businesses are permitted to sell what quality they please and to take what price satisfies their fancy. This strikes me as important.

Indeed, the ex-shareholder may, I observe, lend back to the Canadian Government the very money received for his shares. The Government must borrow it from some one. Why not from the former shareholder? And if such be the case then the Shareholder becomes a Government bond-holder. In place of railway security he receives the bond of the Canadian people; in place of low

"52 QUESTIONS"

return or none at all,* five or six per cent.! Certainly he loses nothing.

NOR will the great General Managers lose money. Obviously their services must still be required by the Government. Changing allegiance from a Board of Directors to the People of Canada may mean for them a depressing psychological change, but no money loss.

---

* On the $60,833,333 of the G.T.R. "Guaranteed" stock a total dividend averaging 2.84% since 1880 has been paid; on the $16,644,000 "1st Preferred" since 1880 a total dividend averaging 3.29% was paid; on the $12,312,666 "2nd Preferred" since 1880 a total dividend averaging 2.45% was paid; on the $34,884,535 "3rd Preferred" since 1880 a total dividend averaging .46 of one per cent. was paid. On the total of $120,682,437 Common Stock actually issued—nothing has been paid.

THIS matter concerns, therefore, the man who owns no railway securities, who earns as much as forty dollars a week, and also his wife, his sister, his mother or his daughter. These, so far as I am able to see, are the only people who run any risk of loss in the nationalization of our railways.

Why am I, the Citizen, Touched Deepest?

BECAUSE my prosperity, like yours, depends on Canada's prosperity;

Because Canada's prosperity depends on the sale of goods;

Because the sale of goods depends, first, upon the cheapness with which a given quality can be offered in the

"52 QUESTIONS"

face of foreign competition; second, upon Speed in Delivery; third, upon Reliability in Delivery.

What Affects Cheap Production?

CHEAPNESS depends on costs, and railway service enters at least five times into the cost of producing Canadian goods:

1. In the cost of freight on raw material to factory.
2. In the cost of freight on other supplies, such as fuel.
3. In the cost of freight in the personal supplies of workers—affecting wages.
4. In the cost of freight from producer to consumer.
5. In taxes incurred on Government railway account.

"52 QUESTIONS"

What Effect has Railway Speed or Reliability on Canadian Business?

MILLIONS of dollars marching into the pockets of workmen in the United States during the winter of 1917-18 were lost, I learn, because the American railroads broke down under strain.

The flow of raw materials to American factories was interrupted.

The escape of the finished goods from the shipping rooms to the shops was prevented.

Deliveries were SLOW.

Promises of delivery became UNRELIABLE.

Orders came to Canada, whose railways had NOT, I find, broken down and whose deliveries were faster and more reliable.

II

May not Railway Nationalization Reduce Railway Costs?

1. *By a central management, as in Great Britain and in the United States?* That centralized management, I discover, has existed in Canada since October, 1917, in the form of the Canadian Railway War Board.

2. *By eliminating duplication of service?* Such elimination has already taken place under that War Board, much to the discomfort of amiable persons who live far from Toronto.

3. *By making one staff do the work of several?* This is not impossible. I can see where, if properly carried out, such an arrangement would be

"5 2 QUESTIONS"

highly economical. Two factors impress one unfavorably, however: first, the universal over-staffing of Government railway departments; and, second, the present under-staffed condition of the private roads due to labor shortage.

4. *By returning to the railway users or to the public Treasury the profits now earned or likely to be earned by private railway companies?* A vitally important point from the citizens' outlook. This, certainly, would be the great desideratum. But investigation and careful scrutiny of the facts lead me to believe that with the reduced efficiency of Government ownership, even at existing rates, there would be no profits to rebate unless the Government, as it does in the case of the

"52 QUESTIONS"

Intercolonial Railway, paid the fixed charges of its roads out of General Revenue and charged the loss to the Canadian tax-payer. That, of course, would save nothing to the tax-payer.

But assume the roads did not lose in efficiency by being brought under Government ownership. Assume that they continued to earn the same yearly average dividend earned by the Grand Trunk and C.P.R. since 1880 and 1883 respectively (the earliest years for which reports are available). There would have been no saving to the Canadian people. The Grand Trunk shareholder has never received more than 5% in any one year (the Canadian Government is now paying 5½% for its borrowings), and on the average, taking

"52 QUESTIONS"

all classes of issued stock into consideration, has received much less than common bank interest. Even with no fall in efficiency the Canadian people would be committing themselves to an annual loss now borne by hopeful shareholders. The Canadian Pacific shareholders have received since 1883 an average of a little less than $7,000,000 a year —larger dividends have apparently been the exception, not the rule— from the operations of the railroad, or say 4% on an investment of $175,000,000. On the basis of the actual physical value of the Canadian Pacific Railway to-day this average yearly dividend would pay nearer two per cent. than four. The Canadian people, borrowing to buy the C.P.R., would have had to pay

"52 QUESTIONS"

the difference between net earnings and the interest charges. At a rate of earning based only on the recent prosperous years of the C.P.R. the calculation would be more favorable to the purchaser—still assuming, of course, that Government management, direct or indirect, would be as efficient as the present management. Even that profit would not make up all the loss on the G.T.R. And if the C.P.R. efficiency fell— what then?

Further: take away the annual bonus paid the Government by the roads in the form of mail carried at less than cost† and officials carried for nothing—consider the reduced alertness, energy and enterprise of the officials which follows their

---
† See pages 113 and 114.

"52 QUESTIONS"

transfer from Private to Public management—and the saved Profit vanishes!

5. *By doing away with the evil of routing goods indirectly?* Here we amateur railroad experts must study geography. This evil has never existed in Canada as it has in Great Britain and in the United States. In most of Canada practically all roads run, I observe, in straight lines, parallel, east and west. The C.P.R., Grand Trunk, or C.N.R., I learn, handle goods between any of their competitive points in practically the same mileage. Unlike Great Britain and the United States, the geographical configuration of the country does not, at the present state of settlement, encourage the building of

"52 QUESTIONS"

triangular railroad routes. Canadian cities, with a few exceptions, tend to lie in a straight line. There is thus no indirect-routing evil to be dealt with!

Or May Not Nationalization Increase Railway Speed?

1. *By routing goods over the shortest line?* According to the reports of the Canadian Railway War Board inter-routing is already in operation under that Board to the fullest possible extent.

2. *By making one road share with another its surplus of locomotive power, or repair facilities, or rolling stock?* This has long since been provided under the War Board whenever necessity demands it.

"52 QUESTIONS"

May Not Nationalization Increase Railway Reliability?

1. *By making all lines co-operate in relieving a congested district?* This is already done, as, for example, when, in the winter of 1917-18, C.P.R., G.T.R., and T. H. & B. all carried coal from the Niagara Frontier to Toronto, and the G.T.R., C.P.R. and C.N.R. carried eastbound goods from Toronto irrespective of the original routing.

2. *By offering the facilities of one road to another, short of facilities?* That also is one of the functions of the Canadian Railway War Board.

"52 QUESTIONS"

**But—
If Nationalization can
do no Good it can do no Harm?**

IN this I believe you err. Nationalization, I am convinced, will shatter in a few years the MORALE now maintained by the privately-owned roads and which is to-day the pace-maker for the Government roads.

III

What is Morale?

IT is the guarantee of that energy, alertness, initiative and enterprise-with-discipline which produces a maximum of result from a *minimum* of staff, with a *minimum* of material in a *minimum* of time.

What does Morale do?

WHAT an automobile tire is without air—that is a nation-wide railway system without Morale.

How can That be?

YOU hear, coming from the vicinity of the railway yards, one stormy night, a rumble of sounds. You visit the yards. . . Very picturesque, you say. Black iron beasts, one eyed, with humps of coal on their backs, move clumsily backward and forward in the railway yards, herding their docile flocks. Others move in from the open road: or out.

Caravans of dripping shadows, you say, marked at the head with an arrogant eye of light, at the tail by a glowing ruby, or an emerald. You observe the laconic twist and turn of signal lamps on ghostly towers. The flash of quick-swung lanterns. Far away the polished main-lines wheel out into the fields, spinning swift smooth paths east and west. Comes from out there the cry of the last out-bound Adventurer, fainter as he thrusts deeper into the night. Near at hand, a silver flicker on a

"52 QUESTIONS"

switchman's dribbling tower . . another Adventurer in-bound through the storm. The rail joints click like castanets ahead of him. The fixed stare of his furious eye silvers the waiting curve and commands ghostly smiles on trackside puddles! He plunges past, great thighs working fast! His rocking caravan in tow looks a pious lot, heads bent, mumbling, under his plume of flame-lit smoke.

Picturesque, you say!

More than that. The rain, mark you, makes the rail slippery. The cold, please observe, makes the steel tire slow to "bite." There has been, therefore, grim work to-night on the heavy grades,—hard firing! Wet, cold jobs cutting long freights in two to climb the hills. Or flagging

"52 QUESTIONS"

thirty poles behind with lamp and torpedoes! Flagging thirty poles ahead—and trudging back to the long wail of the engine.

Tense work in despatchers' offices ordering "meets!" Tense work in the round-houses keeping up with repairs! And in the offices of Superintendents and General Superintendents, working hard to prevent break-downs, or to clear up those which seem inevitable.

Yet this is child's play compared to winter. Twenty-five below, and air leaking from the stiffened couplings! Brakes jammed! A blizzard sucking the steam out of the engine! Snow drifts packing over the rail! Terminals snowed under! Storage tracks full! Main lines jammed!

Here is adventure! And as it is

"52 QUESTIONS"

Morale that in the long run crowns the Adventurer with success whether in a raid across No Man's Land or tiger hunting in Bengal, so it is in the carrying of common goods.

You sell ten cheese for Montreal delivery or bring a crate of eggs from Cousin Lizzie's farm up north. You pay a fee and sign a bill. But part of what you have bought is *pluck!* The spirit and the discipline that make railroads win or fail in the War with Time, with the weakness of men and machines and the devilment of storms.

That is Morale!

Small organizations may not need it; your local street car line; your provincial affair; one man in charge may dominate a staff. But in the

"52 QUESTIONS"

far-scattered organization of national railroads—here fighting snow, there fighting rain, here fighting track trouble, there fighting a sudden rise in the flood of traffic—Morale is life!

What Has Morale To Do With My Town?

THIS:
Two towns lay at equal distances from a great market. Each dominated a rich valley. Down the valleys placid rivers made their way to the market. Each of the towns had about the same population and the same endowment of capital.
One shrivelled and became a joke for the vaudeville actors.
The other grew greater.

"52 QUESTIONS"

THE first was served by a moderately well-run railway. The General Manager of this railway was the nephew of the owner. Like most men whose positions have been *given* not *earned,* he was afraid of the owner.

The latter was wealthy and whimsical. He had not built this railway but had inherited it. His moods and his multiplicity of interests compelled the manager to be cautious of change, to avoid innovation unless the owner asked it. The manager suppressed his own initiative. He studied only to keep his road doing a jog-along business without getting into trouble with the owner.

The changes the owner *did* order were erratic. He had no special desire for dividends. He had numberless

"52 QUESTIONS"

scattered and varied interests, social, political and industrial. He was no more susceptible to the wiles of a smooth talker than any other human being; a good phrase tickled his fancy probably as much as it did any intelligent man—not more. *But* being indifferent to the earnings of the road, *he allowed the smooth talk,* the good phrases, and social and political matters *to influence his view of the railway management.*

Plain railroad facts did not stir him. They made dry reading.

His manager operated the railway on the harum-scarum policy resulting from the owner's divided interests and the inexpert advice of his cronies.

"52 QUESTIONS"

THE railway which served the second town was poor. Its management had just been placed in the hands of a man who had been offered ten thousand shares of stock *and a chance in time to own the road* if he could pull it out of the hole and show a dividend.

" I will," he had said, " provided I have a free hand. Absolutely no interference until I show my balance sheet at the end of the first year."

He cut the dead wood out of the staff. He showed his men that there were rewards, and big rewards, for those who helped make the line a success. He injected some of his own spirit into the staff. He made every man a worker, not just for the road, but for the industries along the road, its customers!

"52 QUESTIONS"

Together, they pulled the road out of the hole.

THE first road gave erratic service. It broke down easily under strain. Its repairs fell behind. The industries in its chief town were sometimes held up for lack of incoming shipments of raw material or for failure of deliveries to get through to customers on time. Protest was vain. Threats were useless. The owner of the road was getting what he thought he wanted out of it—friendships, political pull, amusement of a sort. The industries were finally closed down or sold to second raters. The owner sank his whole fortune trying to mend his broken-down property—and failed.

"52 QUESTIONS"

THE second road turned its chief town into a city by giving crack service and helping the town to capture new industries.

THE first road ruined its territory because its Morale failed. And that happened because its owner had too many scattered interests and was too susceptible to persuasive language.

The Public is just such an owner.

IV

Where does Morale Show Itself?

IN the Section Gang on Section B that must be alert lest the gangs on A and C line-up their curves more skilfully or send the trains more smoothly across the straight stretches.

IN Engineer Carmichael, stalled with leaky boiler tubes, who orders his fires drawn, throws slabs on the hot bars of the furnace, crawls in, with sixty pounds of steam pressure still in the boiler over his head, and caulks his leaking tubes—because he knows " the boss " appreciates that kind of work and depends on him to get this precious train through without calling for help!

"52 QUESTIONS"

IN the Superintendent on Y division, watching his section men, his train crews, his despatching offices, his repair shops for the first sign of failing " pep "—because *his* boss is watching *him*.

IN the General Superintendent of the Middle District, planning or working day by day to cut his grades, reduce his curves, jack up the spirit of his men, in order that *he* may be able to pass trains faster to the Right District and the Left District than they can pass them to him. A football game! War!

IN the General Manager watching the General Superintendents, watching for new General Superintendents, examining expenditures on

"52 QUESTIONS"

fuel, on wages, on claims for goods lost in transit or damaged.

IN the Vice-President holding his departments together.

AND in the President:
"Mr. Vice-President," says he, looking over the skeleton reports, "I see the American roads are handling more traffic per mile of track out of the west than we are. How about it?"
And whatever the explanation, it is the vice-president's business to see that this is no longer the condition. He must find the cause and rout it out. He must re-examine his staff, and transmit down through the ranks to the remotest station agent —more "Pep!"

V

But can the Nationalized Road not have that?

NO. Reluctant as the word may come—No! Down through that quick-nerved staff, ten thousand lads dreaming of the Presidency some day, leaping to obey, will have their *vision* cut off at one stroke—by Nationalization. Full of that quality which everywhere marks the superior breed of men, these boys and men desire to be master of the shop —not clerk, nor even deputy, but able to earn the highest responsibility, the control of that kind of work on the Road! Able to stand, as the Big Boss stands on the pinnacle which nobody *gave* him but which he helped to build and *climbed* himself! Able to say, as every decent man loves to say of his work: "A poor thing, but mine own!"

Young railroad men happy in the consciousness that there is only *one* game they need to know to win even the highest post, Railroading! not Politics—these are the men who make great railroaders.

Nationalization to them means stagnation! Lost ambition!

Lost Confidence! But why should They Feel that Way?

A FINNICKY and unskilled boss —the Public! An uncertain game in which the power of some unknowing newspaper is as likely to have a man fired as not or promoted out of his turn. A game in which the wise man suppresses his

"52 QUESTIONS"

initiative, "sits tight," and "sings small." A game in which "the top" is closed to the worker!

Sentiment! you say?

No. Psychology! Observe the ambitious girl made a household drudge. She hates it because no amount of drudgery can ever make that house or home her own. Make it her own home, cheap, poor and cold—and watch her work!

Yet—Did Morale Save the American Lines from Collapse?

NO. Because, as you will find by a little study, a timid public had sanctioned for years a railway policy which no degree of pluck could save from a disastrous ending. A policy which forbade roads to combine with one another and form transcontinental systems, and which had endowed the country, when war arrived, with seven hundred roads, not one of them able to operate a train from coast to coast.

A policy which forced upon these roads highly competitive conditions which stimulated the indirect-routing evil, fancy and extravagant services, and dubious methods of finance.

A policy which held rates down at a ruinous figure and forced the managements into the hands of Wall Street gamblers, using the properties merely as stock-juggling propositions; or managers who paid dividends and bond interest out of money required for repairs and extensions; and managers who paid miserable wages and offended labor

"52 QUESTIONS"

all because the means to do otherwise were unobtainable.

A policy which in 1917 had left the United States with seven hundred little roads, not one of them National, all inexperienced in transcontinental operation, many in run-down condition.

A policy which McAdoo at once reversed by advancing $222,000,000 for repairs and extensions; by raising freight and passenger rates 40%; by cutting down service to the point of actual discomfort; and by raising wages.

Yet to-day, in spite of easier finances, centralized control and higher wages, *the chief worry of the United States Railway Administration appears to be the falling Morale of the staffs.*

VI

Where Three Men lacked Morale.

THE Despatcher at Jonesville was the first. He lost his nerve, as the railroaders say. The Superintendent was the second. He did not like to "fire" the despatcher. He was his brother-in-law.

The despatcher distrusted his own judgment. To protect himself and the road from the danger of ordering one train to pass another at some impossible point, he made the "up" trains *wait* for the "down" trains at points half-an-hour ahead of the point where they might properly have passed with perfect safety!

In a railway where every man is

"52 QUESTIONS"

working for the promotion, and the best are aiming for "the top," the Superintendent would not have dared retain this despatcher. The low tonnage record over this division would have betrayed him, or the abnormally high coal consumption on his territory would have advertised to the head office that something was wrong. Explanations would have shown up the nerveless despatcher.

But on a system in which the desire for profits (after the requirements of the law have been met) was *not* constantly sharpening the eyes of the High Executives, the low tonnage and the high fuel cost were obscured by other considerations. It is true that one man, an auditor,

"52 QUESTIONS"

noted the fuel charges against that division, but decided silence would pay him better than enquiry. The matter was not *strictly* in his department, and he had found there was nothing to be gained on *that* road by being "a disturber." His position was secure at least until there was a change in Government. "Why trouble Trouble?" He was the third!

FIVE years earlier—before the auditor, like the despatcher and the superintendent, had lost his pep, he would have sat up nights trying to find the reason for the high fuel consumption. Then he would have acted, promptly, curtly. But he had learned the Philosophy of the Civil Servant everywhere:

"52 QUESTIONS"

"Of *what use is striving? Or of asserting one's opinions? It is a vulgar thing which upsets other people who desire to be comfortable! It draws attention to oneself which, in a servant of the public, is highly undignified and perchance dangerous. The public is a jealous and an uncertain tempered employer, whose ears are numberless, whose interests are legion, who has no expert experience enabling him to judge your work, but is infinitely sensitive, imaginative and susceptible to the dangerous power of smooth words. It is better then, O Civil Servant, in the interests of one's place and one's family to be a master of tact and words than a master of one's work."*

"52 QUESTIONS"

Rewards?
Or Responsibilities?

THE newly-appointed Section Foreman at B had been a farmer and had rendered excellent political service to the local member of Parliament in the 1917 election, leaving the farm for his boys to look after. He had helped his M.P. to swing into line a number of malcontents whose rebellion against the party machine threatened to defeat the member and weaken the Government at a time when the very highest interests of the country demanded nation-wide support.

He had done *good* and *necessary* work; nothing dishonorable about it. Returning to his farm, however, he found that two fine calves from the prize stock had died owing to lack of attention. They had been born just about the time he was busy helping the M.P. Here, then, was an honest man injured in public service! He was losing interest in the farm, too. By giving up his cattle-breeding hobby he could leave the farm to the boys alone. What he ought to have, he felt, was "a job." He was made section foreman, instructed in the work, and put on the pay roll of this railway.

ONE year later, looking over the records of the road, the General Manager observed an unusually high number of derailments charged against the Patriot's section.

"There's Gilhooly's curve right there," he remembered; "a nasty

"52 QUESTIONS"

curve—but this looks like bad track work. Alignment on that curve should have kept things right."

He called a clerk, and dictated a wire to the Superintendent. The Superintendent, passing down the line, called on the Patriot and gave him, in railroad parlance, Hell!

BUT the Patriot remembered the cattle he had sacrificed. Righteous indignation flushed his cheek—why not? He went to his M.P. The M.P. addressed the General Manager. The General Manager, *nominally controlled by a non-political Board, but knowing well that the M.P. could put in a good or a bad word for him with the Public if his work were ever discussed in Parliament,* gave the Patriot another post.

While the Patriot could not now wreck trains, he still remained inefficient. He was a simple, honest man. He was as indifferent to the new as to the old work. What the Patriot thought he had earned was *reward,* not responsibility.

THERE will be thousands upon thousands of such men in Canada in the next few years; and of real patriots who will deserve much better of their country than mere berths on Government railways.

Where Initiative Died.

IN a certain engine repair shop was a machine for planing the driving boxes of engines. It consisted of a gigantic steel table or

"52 QUESTIONS"

carrier made to hold ten boxes at a time and to roll them slowly up toward the second part of the machine consisting of two cutting tools which cut into the brass and trimmed the boxes. The machine was operated by an electric motor. The motor consumed the same amount of power whether ten boxes lay on the steel table or only one.

Under an indifferent shop superintendent the machine was more often worked with one box on it than with ten. A man wanted a box planed? He carried it up on the electric travelling crane, lowered it on the table, turned on the power—and used on one box the power that would have planed ten.

A NEW OFFICIAL, keen, filled with ideals and the belief that his highest ambition was to serve the Public—observed this wasteful practice, rated the superintendent for his slackness, and ordered a change made.

Months passed. The official returned and made the same fuss—and nothing came of it. The superintendent had an uncle who was chairman of an organization which controlled the vote in a certain very ticklish constituency—and until human nature is greatly improved NO Government, however pure, can afford to overlook the very practical and sometimes sordid things which win elections.

The loss on the operation of the machine was perhaps small. But

"52 QUESTIONS"

the effect on the officer who tried to save that small loss was *great*. It was *his* first lesson in the Philosophy of the Government employee.

IDEAS, I observe, have a harder birth in Government offices than anywhere else in the world. Initiative must indeed have great pertinacity and courage to survive service in a Government department.

VII

What makes Morale?

MORALE is a combination of two opposites.

First: Spirit.

Second: Discipline.

A body of men all Discipline lacks initiative, resilience, resourcefulness, "come-back." A body all Spirit cannot long remain organized. Spirit is the horse; Discipline the harness. The ideal is the lightest possible harness with the swiftest possible horse.

So in the great organizations of railways scattered, as they lie, across thousands of miles of territory, varied in climate, industry, interest and topography.

"52 QUESTIONS"

What Provides the Spirit in Morale?

FIVE things, I think, provide the element of Spirit:

"A's" hope of earning more money.
"B's" desire for greater authority and more money. "C's" ambition to be the head! To be master! To control the organization!

"D" asks only the satisfaction of duty done.

"E" asks only to be allowed to serve his country.

"D" and "E" must be eliminated at once. They may be excellent men, but the calculations of great organizations carrying on prosaic businesses in Peace time or in War time cannot be based on exceptional and accidental men. They must, I conclude, be based on "A," "B" and

"C." These three men respond to universal, constant, and reliable motives to which wise managements know how to appeal.

"A's" desire to earn more money is common to all. It affects the workman, the private in the ranks, as well as the officer.

"B" and "C" are usually of the officer class, or are potentially officials.

"B," to earn the greater authority for which he craves, realizes that he must prove himself able to "hold" his men. Must know their work and know their tools. Must apply the principles of leadership. Otherwise he has strikes on his hands, or inefficient work.

"C," seeking promotion, must show, in addition to "B's" qualities, resourcefulness in overcoming difficulties, invention in improving the means of labor, alertness in anticipating trouble, energy in forestalling it,—and judgment! Thus in "A," "B" and "C" I observe the working of Spirit.

But Spirit is Easily Quenched?

PRECISELY! Spirit dies unless the ambitious worker is confident that if he manifests good qualities they will be recognized by some officer higher up.

Spirit dies if the worker feels that the officer with the responsibility has yet not the full power to reward.

Spirit dies if the worker finds he is not to be judged by a single known standard, that is for merit, and merit as a railroader only, but for

"52 QUESTIONS"

other considerations, and on outside standards of judgment. At this point the worker stops and the wire-puller begins.

So far three conditions, you observe. But the fourth is most essential. The " top " must be open. The ultimate rewards in sight must be adequate to the man. Your potential member of the firm does not long remain in a concern that will never yield him a partnership. The brighter your servant the more eagerly she aspires to some other work where she may some day be her own proprietor. The potentially great railway expert does not long remain in a system where " the top " is closed, where the highest posts and final authorities are for appointees of Parliament, not railroaders.

He goes to private service—in the armies of generals whom he *may* dream of succeeding!

What Provides Discipline?

DISCIPLINE is obtained, of course, by withholding reward, or delaying it, or by discharge. It must be administered by men (1) competent to judge, (2) to judge fairly, (3) to judge by single known standards, and (4) to put their judgment into effect.

VIII

Cannot a Government Manager Observe These Conditions for Preserving Morale?

IT is possible that all of the officers giving rewards in each department may be skilled railway men capable of judging.

IT is possible that their judgments will be as fair as in any other railway.

IT is possible that their rewards and punishments, when issued on the merits of a case and merit only, may not be over-ruled.

"52 QUESTIONS"

IT is possible that a single standard of judgment, namely, ability as a railroad servant, may be maintained—and that considerations of a political nature will not enter in.

But it is *not* possible to climb to "the top." The "top" is closed! The current of life in the whole organization is sluggish. Any sincere, practical-minded Canadian who has had any experience in business life, or who has observed the face and the philosophy of the average civil servant in Canada or anywhere else, knows, though his memory may still echo the fine-sounding pledges of sentimental politicians, that the man still good for inspired, creative work, shuns a Government department.

"52 QUESTIONS"

The most necessary stimulant to the ablest young officials, the lure of the open "top," the subconscious hope of one day being *master* of the department, or even of the whole organization—is missing, and can never be provided.

The "top" is now a political affair in the gift of the hardest master in the world—the Public! To retain one's enthusiasm and initiative and yet please a public that not merely commands certain standards of service through the Railway Commission but *owns* one body and soul, is a problem that not even the hardiest politician could undertake with any hope.

"52 QUESTIONS"

The Hardest Master in the World?

IS ourselves—the Public! The wisest of judges *after* the event! The poorest of judges before, or at the time of the event.

Statesmen, the devoted students of the Public mind, more often die broken-hearted than not, through the hastiness or slow understanding of their public.

The politicians most astute, often miscalculate its will, and suffer its punishment.

DIVIDED in its viewpoint,—
Diverse in its interests,—
With many standards to satisfy,—
With an ear ever quicker for the catch-phrase than the reasoned

"52 QUESTIONS"

argument,—The public is the hardest master in the world!

With a special court to interpret the public to the roads and the roads to the public—each is protected. Without such protection the ablest railroader may be overthrown by a catch-phrase and the wiliest demagogue enthroned—through a newspaper cartoon. Good men will avoid such service.

IX

But—
War Has Changed the Public?

IN some things!

If in the exalted mood which war sustained in the Public there were still inefficient departments at Ottawa, still partisanship, still seekers after patronage—and there *were*—men need not hope for better in the inevitable reaction *after* the War. The exalted mood will not long remain to sustain us.

What then?

One form of Government, and one form only, can be efficient in executive matters: Bureaucracy because it boasts a suppressed and controlled public opinion. Democracy with its free public opinion is inevitably inefficient in executive matters. It has a loftier function, a higher goal, slow to attain, and not to be abandoned for the mere whim of the Nationalizers.

But the Government Will Place the Railways out of Politics!

THAT does not answer the prime objection just pointed out: the owner remains the same, the capricious, sensitive, imaginative public. And "the top" is closed. No ambitious young officers will dream of becoming master of *this* road. It is everybody's road and therefore no one's!

"52 QUESTIONS"

**But—
We Shall Appoint a Commission of Business Men!**

WHAT a naive confession of our faith in Private enterprise rather than Public enterprises to develop great executives!

Why has the Intercolonial Railway not one senior executive developed from within itself?

Why are critics always saying that "we should get business men into the Government?"

Why is the field for developing executives *outside,* not inside, the executive departments of Government?

Why do most of the efficient men, once in the executive department of Government service, seem to dwindle at once into numb-faced Civil servants?

Because they have already run their course and spent the impetus of their youthful ambition in private service.

And because, if they have a spark of it left, they miss the old freedom! The thrill of creating for themselves with their own hands, uninterrupted so long as they obey the law.

"The top" is closed and the caprice of a democratic Public breaks—nine times out of ten—the spirit.

For the man coming *in* or for the man coming *up* the most significant elements in the situation are these: First, a capricious master; a master whom one cannot hope, by any degree of patience and worth, to succeed; second, a closed "top."

"52 QUESTIONS"

The Case of the Rajah.

A RAJAH bought, let us say, incense for his temples from a mud-walled factory owned by a Jew and manned by diligent Chinese boys. The price of incense and the quality were both fixed by a special officer of the court.

On the advice of a fakir, who disapproved of the Jew's religion—and profit, the rajah bought out the business and made one of the noblest courtiers in the land its manager.

Yet within a year, though the boys were beaten and threatened, and coaxed and bribed—the quality of the incense fell away.

The old incentive was removed. The best boys, those who had dreamed of succeeding the Jew some day and of being known in the bazaar as Yo

"52 QUESTIONS"

Shin the Maker of Incense, knew now there was no longer such a possibility. The "top" was closed. To be known even as Master of the Rajah's Incense Rooms was outside their scope. They were incense-makers, not politicians.

THERE is a second part to this parable:
The rajah finally dismissed the old nobleman and sent far and wide for the men highest in the incense trade.

One said: " I am getting tired of my own business. I have got all that I want. I would like some public honors." So *he* accepted.

Another said: " I would like to let my grandchildren remember me as an officer of the Rajah. My

"52 QUESTIONS"

business will take care of itself." And *he* went.

A third said: "I'm getting old, and I've lost a lot of money on the camel races lately. I guess I'd better get in out of the cold." So *he* went.

But not *one* of them went with the enthusiasm once given his own little struggling business!

And in time, the First wearied of the Rajah's whims and resigned.

The Second was beheaded for grafting.

The Third "laid low." He needed the money!

Meanwhile the ablest of the Chinese boys vanished to start incense industries—*of—their—own!*

X

Who are the Nationalizers?

A FEW sincere Canadians.

Why do They Seem so Numerous?

FOR four reasons:
First: They include a number of newspaper editors whose voices are multiplied through the art of printing.
Second: The discontented and dissatisfied who exist in every country echo their language with vague approval. The policy of " Nationalization " offers them, not a cure for the abuses they deplore—and deplore perhaps rightly—but a distraction.

"52 QUESTIONS"

Third: The prospect of despoiling the rich and overthrowing the successful has been a popular proposal among the less intelligent people since the earliest days of the race. Although the leaders of the Nationalization movement may not—do not—intend their arguments to inflame unwholesome passions, such, nevertheless, is one effect of their campaign.

Fourth: The other side is silent or speaks foolishly. The old-time railway magnate with his bluff and cajolery is gone. The modern managers are pathetically afraid to speak.

Those newspaper owners and editors who might in their hearts be convinced that Nationalization was dangerous, require great courage to say so, for they will promptly be accused of being in the hire of the "interests."

In short, there is a premium on any sort of argument in favor of Public Ownership and a penalty on its counterpart.

That is why the few seem so many.

What do They Mean by Nationalization?

THE Purchase of all Canadian railways. Bear the word in mind—"Purchase!"

Is That What the Americans Did?

NO. They guaranteed the continuance of earnings to shareholders and created a central railroad directorate equivalent to the

"52 QUESTIONS"

Canadian Railway War Board to co-ordinate the roads and to remove the wasteful competition which the United States, like Great Britain, had long insisted upon. *They did not Purchase* the railroad systems which they now are operating!

Did the British Government Buy out the British Roads?

NO. It eliminated wasteful competitive conditions as the Americans did by guaranteeing earnings and establishing central control equivalent to the Canadian Railway War Board. *It did not Purchase* the railroad systems. The British, like the Americans, are still far from taking the step advocated by the "Nationalizers" in Canada.

"52 QUESTIONS"

Why not do Precisely as They Did?

BECAUSE, so far as I can see, it is totally unnecessary. Competitive conditions are not in any sense the same in Canada. The guaranteeing of earnings would merely pass a burden to Canada without any compensating gain.

XI

Where, Then, Does the Movement Begin?

FIRST: in a feeling of dislike for "the railroads."

The early history of the roads is heroic, but not, I think, morally beautiful. Perhaps it could not have been much different. In my experience your man of even-handed justice and unswerving loyalty to the highest code of ethics never has, never does, never can, without altering his nature, blast out new paths of enterprise. Railroads were one of the earliest manifestations of organized Capital. Capital like any other great force or power—like rivers, tides, steam, electricity, opiates, young horses, kings, children, or organized labor—has to be tamed!

The railroads had their fling, but they are nearer under sound control in Canada than is any other department of Capital. And meantime, to my way of thinking, their former excesses have not one single thing to do with Nationalization!

Foolish charters? Monopolies such as that of the Toronto Street Railway? Privileges such as the railroads had before they were brought under the Dominion Railway Commission? Unregulated services? Unregulated rates? These iniquities must disappear from all departments of business enterprise as they have disappeared from the Canadian railroads. But on the railways

"52 QUESTIONS"

these things *have* been settled: and prudent citizens do not confuse the old dead issues with the new.

A Parable.

CONSIDER it this way: A certain village languished because the dams thrown across the river at that point were again and again swept away by floods and the millers ruined. The villagers sought a man who would build a dam strong enough to hold the river, and a substantial mill that would bring traffic through the village for all time to come.

He appeared.

But the qualities which made him successful in building the proper sort of dam—his cunning, his determination, his tenacity of purpose applied equally to his activities among the people. In their first eagerness to obtain the benefits of his qualities they allowed him to obtain the position of an overlord and oppressor.

Long after he had been tamed and was indeed dead, those whom he had injured or offended remembered his iniquities against his son. The son was a law-abiding man, and confined himself to making the mill a success. But seeing the wealth which the miller had amassed from the mill they felt suddenly that the village should take back the site on the shore of the river which had been donated to encourage the old miller in the first place.

" No," said others, " that would be confiscation, and it would soon

"52 QUESTIONS"

apply to everybody's business. Let us buy out the mill and get rid of the son."

They bought the mills and in time were ruined—not because Public Ownership of a mill must necessarily fail, but because the whole basis of their action had been spite! Resentment and malice had led them where business judgment should have shown a better way.

Nationalization of Canadian Railways is in danger of being decided as unwisely.

But—
What About Land Grants?

THE history of Canada includes some very unpleasant records of public lands and public moneys thrown away. The whole of the public lands of Prince Edward Island were given away in one day. The famous estates of some of the best known Ontario families were based on land grants obtained by "pull."

Let us assume there was no justification for railway land grants. Take the most hostile view of the matter.

Let the Dominion of Canada enter action to recover such lands if it feels that course to be right.

But keep the two issues clear!

The newspaper or public speaker who drags these matters into the discussion of the railways of Canada and their proposed Nationalization is guilty of an attempt to take the public mind away from the real issue, and of using foul means, even unpatriotic means, to move his constituency to endorse him and his policy.

**But—
the Existence of Great Corporations Menaces the Purity
of Our Legislators!**

CORRUPTION is possible so long as Governments are corruptible.

The corruption of legislatures by railways is much less likely to occur and much easier detected and punished than that corruption of both Parliament and the railways, which, if our Governments cannot be trusted, must very rapidly follow Nationalization.

The policeman corrupt enough to bargain with a burglar is surely not to be given a cash box!

"52 QUESTIONS"

Fear of the "influence" of the wealthy corporations at Ottawa is not the least of the primary motives of the "Nationalizers." But surely no more pathetic reason for wishing Nationalization has yet been advanced for placing in the hands of corruptible men—if they remain corruptible—such temptation as more Nationalized railways.

XII

What Raises the Question of Nationalization Now?

THREE THINGS:

First: The financial collapse of the Canadian Northern and the financial difficulties of the Grand Trunk Pacific. The Canadian Northern is now on the Government's hands. The Grand Trunk Pacific may have to be taken over.

Second: The increases in railway rates allowed by the Government in order to meet the extraordinary increases in wages and the cost of supplies.

Third: The example of England and the United States.

What has the C.N.R. to do with the Question of Buying Other Roads?

IT appears—nothing.

As the result of rash public sentiment some years ago, and Government stupidity, Ottawa now finds itself compelled to own the C.N.R. in order to save Canada's credit. It is a misfortune which surely cannot be construed into an argument for *further* purchases! Examine it closely and you will observe that it is in itself the finest possible evidence of a democratic Government's business simplicity. It does not matter what party may then have been in power. The errors of Ottawa Governments do not fall to the exclusive credit of either side.

"52 QUESTIONS"

**But—
the Government is Left with
Only the Roads that Cannot Succeed?**

THIS is scarcely true. I find, on making thorough enquiry, that if Public Ownership wishes to experiment with a national railway system it has now every physical essential. It taps a better farming area in the west, has easier grades in the Rockies, better curves and grades and richer country along the North Shore of Lake Superior, and exclusive direct connection with Halifax.

The argument that such a system cannot succeed without the old Grand Trunk being added savors of insincerity. Is it possible the

"52 QUESTIONS"

Nationalizers are preparing excuses already?

Even if this were not so there would still be no argument for Nationalization. *The losing roads would lose no less because they were Nationalized.* The paying roads would, I am only too sure, cease to pay and deteriorate.

G.T.R. shareholders now pay the interest on the capital stock—that is to say, they get no dividends, and therefore their money works for no interest. Bought out, it must *then* be the Canadian people who shall pay that interest. Money *must* earn a wage. The private shareholder of the G.T.R. is at present paying it; that is, he remits it; he does without it. When his holdings are bought out by a Government that

Government must pay interest on the money borrowed for the purchase. (*See footnote to page* 7.)

**But—
Consider the Rate Tangle!**

I HAVE considered this carefully, and this is what I find:
Prior to 1904 railway rates were limited only by competitive conditions (where they existed) and by a few vague restrictions in the Railway Act. The railways used and abused their liberty in much the same way that your child or mine, or the Manufacturers' Association or the banks or any live human being will abuse power if improperly controlled. In the west were exhibited all the evils of an unregulated monopoly—precisely the sort of

thing that the "Nationalizers" are craving.

In 1904 the Dominion Board of Railway Commissioners was appointed. It provided a special court to hear complaints against railways cheaply and quickly. It was to be, and is, the judge of what is good service and what is bad. Rates are fixed by this court absolutely. They do not merely approve; they set the rates.

IN 1918 this body, I find, allowed two rate increases: a first increase nominally described as 15%, and applying to both freight and passenger rates. According to the railways this did not, however, mean an increase of 15% in the gross income of the roads, but rather about

"52 QUESTIONS"

10%, owing to the fact that rates on certain important commodities were protected by fixed "maximums," preventing the roads from collecting a full 15% increase on such commodities. For this reason the new addition to the gross returns of the roads amounted, they say, to about 10%. I am inclined to believe their statement.

In July, 1918, labor unrest led the roads, through the Canadian Railway War Board, to apply the McAdoo scale of wages as applied in the United States. To do this they deemed it necessary to obtain from the Dominion Railway Commission a further rate increase calculated to yield another 25% addition to their gross income.

"52 QUESTIONS"

This application was decided, not by the Railway Commission, but by the Cabinet. The Railway Commission advised granting the increase on the grounds that fuel had doubled in price, ties doubled, and labor doubled since 1914. It urged that without this increase the weaker railways would be driven to the wall. The Cabinet accepted this view.

The Case of the C.P.R.

HERE rose the difficulty.

To exempt the C.P.R. from the new rate was impossible, as it would drive business from the C.P.R.'s competitors. The C.P.R. must be given the new rates in such a way as to add nothing to its profits— profits due to its initial endowment in public lands, its economical construction and efficient operation. The order was entered, therefore, that any addition to the normal profit of the C.P.R. should be absorbed by the Government, the percentage left to the C.P.R. being designed to act, like the fragment of carrot in the dragoman's hand, to provide the donkey with incentive.

Is That Not Simple Enough?

"NO," says the "Nationalizer," "we cannot trust the Government to carry out the letter of the law. We cannot trust the Government!—any Government! We must 'nationalize' the C.P.R.!"

How, then, is a Government or any body of men to be trusted with the entire railway system of Canada if the same Government cannot be

"52 QUESTIONS"

trusted to collect a tax? Or with the disposition of 147,000 "jobs" without fear or favor? With the prudent extension of lines or alterations in train service in the face of popular demands here and there? With millions of dollars and millions of patrons—many in a position to favor the Government?

If the Government cannot be trusted to "regulate," how can it be trusted to *operate* the roads!

XIII

But Why Have Great Britain and the United States Assumed Temporary Control of Their Roads?

WAR conditions compelled Great Britain and the United States to ensure the shortest and quickest possible routing for traffic. If one road had a shorter route between two points, but lacked equipment which some other road possessed—the second road's equipment must serve on the first road's line.

But in countries having—unlike Canada—depth as well as width, this first road had long been accustomed to maintain its business connections by accepting shipments which another road could carry by a shorter route. In the highly-competitive conditions prevailing in

"52 QUESTIONS"

Great Britain and the United States, no railway could agree to the Government's proposals without having some guarantee against loss. In the United States the problem was more difficult owing to the run-down state of many of the properties and the fact that with 700 railways the Americans possessed *not one* transcontinental organization.

The British and American roads were *not* "Nationalized" in the sense of the word known in Canada, that is, by purchase. The British and American Governments wiped out the need for competition by guaranteeing for the time being the earnings, and ordered their respective roads to work together, letting whoever get the most trade who could best handle it. The same

"52 QUESTIONS"

effect is obtained in Canada with less expense through the Canadian Railway War Board.

Are Our Canadian Roads Working as Efficiently?

QUITE. Studying the maps I observed that Canada, being wide and shallow, her rail connections lie practically east and west. This is a most important consideration. Indirect routing existed, therefore, only in Ontario and in International traffic. The Canadian Railway War Board removed the evil in Ontario and with the co-operation of the McAdoo Railway Administration in the United States eliminated it also in international movements.

Canadians, in my judgment, have reason to be proud of the fact that they had been in the war for four years, had handled 500,000 soldiers, 85,000 coolies, and millions of tons of special war traffic all out of two "and a half" ocean ports without a hitch! The only break-downs were winter tie-ups of a local nature, due partly to the loss of Canadian freight cars in the American breakdown, and partly to the scarcity of workmen for repairing rolling stock. The Canadian Railway War Board, a voluntary association of railways made at the Government's suggestion, perfected this co-operation, already made easy, as I have intimated, by the fact that the Canadian lines are all organized on Transcontinental lines, all running east and west, and competing only in quality of service.

XIV

Is Public Ownership, Then, Always a Failure?

CERTAINLY NOT.
There are circumstances in which, to my way of thinking, it is necessary and logical.

(1) In combatting arrogant monopolies whose charters have not expired and who can be dealt with in no other way.*

(2) When the work to be done is of a special, confidential nature—such as the carrying of mail, the keeping of records and the care of Government property, or the government of subject races as in India.†

---
*It is cheaper to refrain from establishing monopolies, private or otherwise.

† India is, of course, a Bureaucracy.

"52 QUESTIONS"

(3) When the work is purely routine, requiring disinterestedness and dignity rather than alertness, enterprise, resourcefulness.

(4) When the service to be rendered lies within *one* locality, with *one* standard of judgment, capable of being applied by any one in the community (such as street railway or waterworks systems).

(5) When public opinion is muzzled and powerless—in a Bureaucracy such as Prussia once was.

PUBLIC ownership has probably *three* chances of success in an old, thickly populated country to *one* in a young, sparsely-settled country such as Canada.

"52 QUESTIONS"

Where men are crowded together opportunities for employment are likely to be scarce. The opportunity to satisfy personal ambition in private enterprise is limited. A large percentage of the young and ambitious cannot find careers in private business and are glad to fall back on Civil Service employment.

For the ambitious man Civil Service is everywhere in democratic countries *second choice!* Only in Germany is it First. As a rule in this Canada only the weakling, the man with a social ambition or the seeker after an easy berth really wishes to enter the Civil Service.

In Canada private enterprise can and for many a year will have first choice of the men. It offers " the open top," the possibility of becoming master! Civil service gets the men who are left over.

THE army is an exception to the rule. The business of dealing in wounds and death overawes the politician. A leader in the field is above and beyond public control until some disaster or serious breakdown calls for investigation. His successor at once assumes the same freedom from control. The morale of armies, moreover, is the morale of destruction, not construction, the morale of *spending,* not the morale of *maintaining* and *conserving.* Armies in peace times (except in a Bureaucratic State like Germany) tend to go the way of all departments of Civil Service. Red tape

"52 QUESTIONS"

flourishes. Initiative and enterprise die prompt deaths.

LASTLY: exceptional men sometimes occur who are able to combine great executive ability with political ability. But almost invariably they get into the business thus controlled *from the political end*, not from below. "The top" in such organizations is closed!

Personal affection for an exceptional politician, as in the case of Sir Adam Beck in Toronto, may, for the time being, inspire in his officers enthusiasm equal to that in a well-conducted private corporation. Though "the top" is closed they work long and hard for this striking figure who is able to do with the public—at present—what he pleases.

"52 QUESTIONS"

Great railways and their public cannot rely, for cheapness of service, speed and reliability—for alertness, enterprise, energy, initiative—year after year and generation after generation on the accidental occurrence of a great personality.

In old countries,
In armies in war time,
In certain classes of work,
And under exceptional men—
Public Ownership ventures may and do often succeed.

The conditions in the management of railways are different: they promise only calamitous failure.

But what about the State Railways of Germany, Austria, Belgium, France and Australia?

TWO factors make the German, Austrian and Belgian conditions incomparable to Canadian conditions.

1st. The great density of population has three favorable effects on those foreign roads: (*a*) It produces finished or nearly finished materials along every mile of line. The roads haul, therefore, high class commodities over short distances. (*b*) It provides plenty of labor at low wages—lower in Germany before the war than in England. (*c*) The heavy population provides more young, ambitious men than can find careers in private enterprise. Great numbers remain available, therefore,

"52 QUESTIONS"

for Government service—the treadmill of the less ambitious all the world over.

2nd. These countries are under Bureaucratic Government or "Government by officials." (See *last chapter*.)

THE State railways of France, in spite of dense population and dense traffic, had a doubtful record prior to the war. At least as many critics condemned the French State railways as approved them.

THE same is true of the Australian railroads. Quality of service, rates and net earnings, when studied together, show for the Australian roads a very uncertain "success."

"52 QUESTIONS"

What About the Canadian Post Office? Three Cents on a Letter Carries it to the Ends of the Earth! That is Public Ownership! And it Pays!

IT is, first of all, fair to judge the Post Office by the same standards that a bank manager would use in judging *your* business if you wanted a loan.

It should be.

Is it fair that in reckoning the alleged profits of your business the bank should insist on knowing your *real* costs, including any portion which your father, uncle, brother or grandfather may have paid as a gift for you?

"52 QUESTIONS"

Obviously.

That is, if I show a profit selling cordwood at ten dollars a cord because I am able to buy it at five dollars less than *it actually costs* my rich grandfather to produce—and another merchant just comes out even selling at fifteen dollars a cord, *that,* you admit, is no special credit to my skill in merchandising?

Clearly.

That, then, is the position of the Canadian Post Office when credit is claimed for it on the grounds of economical or profitable operation. According to an exhibit * before the

---
* "*Exhibit B, Board of Railway Commissioners of Canada, reference as to compensation for carriage of mails; comparison of Mail Rates with those on other branches of traffic.*"

"52 QUESTIONS"

Dominion Railway Commission the Post Office pays only a nominal rate for the carriage of mail, a rate less than cost. The Canadian traveller and shipper pay the difference.

"A carload of mail," said the document referred to, "moving from Montreal to Ottawa would bring the railway a revenue of $17.76, or, for a ten-ton load one and six-tenth cents a ton-mile (a mile per ton), and *this* for a movement on a high speed passenger train."

On the other hand:

"A car of first class freight," said the document, "with a minimum of ten tons load, moving between Montreal and Ottawa, would bring a revenue of $74.00, or 6.67 cents a ton-mile, *and this for movement on a freight train at freight train speed.*"

"52 QUESTIONS"

Further:

"A carload of parcels post moving between Montreal and Ottawa with a minimum of ten tons to the car would yield the Government $1,280, or $11.53 per car mile (per mile per car) as against $17.76, or sixteen (16) cents a car mile that the Railways would receive for the haulage. *Based on the English system of remuneration the railway would receive $704.00, or $6.34 a car mile.*"

"A special mail train moving between Montreal and Ottawa would yield $1.25 a train mile, or $138.75.

"A special passenger train between Montreal and Ottawa at a minimum charge of $2.50 a mile could not yield less than $280. This might be

"52 QUESTIONS"

increased materially by the number of tickets over the required minimum."

IF the Canadian Post Office was on a par with other businesses—would it *then* really pay?

Is the Canadian Post Office making a high enough profit considering these advantages?

May not two cents or three cents be, in reality, an absurdly *high* rate compared to what it might be if the Post Office was efficiently run?

Is the Canadian Post Office, then, such a sure success as to be cited in support of Railway Nationalization?

XV

How Does the Employee Stand Under Public Ownership?

In pay probably *high*.

In discipline probably *easy*.

In matters of promotion, *badly*, unless he play the toady.

In case of wage dispute—*handicapped*. He has now no disinterested third party, no regulating authority to which he can appeal. He is the servant of the highest authority, one capable of imprisoning him, dismissing him, or declaring him a rebel and an outlaw.

In the course of the Post Office "strike" the following was part of a despatch appearing in the Toronto papers Monday morning, July 29th:

"52 QUESTIONS"

"Hon. Mr. Doherty, Minister of Justice and acting Prime Minister, wired to the secretaries of Boards of Trade (in part) as follows: 'The reasons for objection on the part of the Government to appoint a conciliation board are that it is obviously impossible for the Government to hand over its functions to any outside body. One of the executive functions of the Government is to carry on the public service in accordance with the decisions of Parliament.'"

The Government is no longer a disinterested regulating authority! Whether it concedes or declines to yield a point in discussion with its direct employees depends—not on the actual justice of the case but upon the political effect, direct and indirect, to be expected from its judgment.

How Does Government Ownership Affect the Shipper?

IT deprives him of a disinterested court of appeal such as now exists in the Dominion Railway Commission.

The Commission becomes, under public ownership, a sister department of the railway against whom redress might be desired.

The shipper's servant—the railway—holds at the same time supreme power over him.

Adjustment to railway service will be made with a view to political effect, not the fair interests of all classes and all sections of the country.

How Would Government Ownership Affect Regions Seeking Railway Extension or Betterment?

THE district with many votes on the Government side would tend to obtain everything it asked,—whether justified by business conditions or not.

The districts without political power would help foot the bill.

XVI

Nationalization and Democracy.

IT can take nothing away from our pride and confidence in Democracy, to hold, as this book holds, that the management of railways lies outside the number of things which Democracy, in its present state of development, does well.

IF this book repeats the charge that Democracy,—great in the making of laws, incomparable in the administration of justice, indispensable in developing, generation after generation, something nearer the ideal type of world citizen, is yet pitifully weak in matters of executive nature, and must be so for many generations, it is because there is nothing really discreditable to Democracy in the charge.

THE executive weakness of Democracy is the surest guarantee of that magnificent individualism which helped to make Foch's armies greater than Hindenburg's. It is part of the very genius of Democracy, and something of which your true Democrat—not the panicky, fair-weather friend of Democracy who asks for Bureaucracy, because Bureaucracy is, forsooth, more "efficient"—approves with quiet, knowing, inner satisfaction.

NO opportunity should be missed of reminding ourselves that our old Democratic usages were suspended, not abandoned in the

"52 QUESTIONS"

interests of war-time unity of control and speed of decision. Those frightened "democrats" who clamor to enthrone the State as rival to the individual in business—*master* of industry instead of *regulator* of industry—are in reality capitulating to the very thing our armies fought: Bureaucracy. We have modified our old conception of Individualism. War has quickened our consciousness of mutual interdependence within Nation and Empire. But Democracy remains the Ideal.

AND that is the great difference: Democracy is an Ideal; Bureaucracy a condition.

Democracy a movement, an evolution toward an ideal; Bureaucracy a fixed affair!

"52 QUESTIONS"

Democracy an unfolding from within, a growth from the soil upward: Bureaucracy something stamped upon the community from the top!

Democracy producing many men, tending to grow better in type and in conditions with every generation: Bureaucracy producing supermen—and dupes.

Democracy by its blunders and its allotment of responsibility to everyone, tending to teach every individual the lessons of their combined mistakes: Bureaucracy, concentrating responsibility, leaving the rank and file, as Bismarck himself admitted, "infants in political sense."

"52 QUESTIONS"

THE Democratic State is not designed to do business! It is contrived to foster the growth of the individual within the brotherhood, to reflect and focus in Parliament the experiences of the brotherhood, to deduce from these experiences new laws, or amend old ones, to administer these laws, to "regulate" individual enterprise.

These things does your true Democratic Government and fends off hotly from every side those other things which tend to weaken its disinterestedness.

THAT it might *own*, for the brotherhood, those resources upon which the citizens depend for employment—land, minerals, forests, waters—is a piece of radical

"52 QUESTIONS"

thinking not all inconsistent with the nature and powers of Democracy. That it should extend the principle of regulation to other industries such as farming, manufacturing, wholesaling and retailing quite as thoroughly as it now does to railways—that it might even improve the control now exercised over the railways, is not at all impossible under the principles of real Democracy.

But Nationalization of Railways is an unnecessary and a mischievous extension of the executive side of Democracy. The Government becomes then no longer the disinterested Judge and Regulator. It is made a servant and yet Master. A competitor and yet an overlord! A servant above and beyond all direct control outside itself. The Government ceases to be the plastic coat, described by Anatole France, which continually alters as the people develop, and never tears! It tends to become, instead, a Bureaucracy!

Could anything, then, be more absurd and mischievous than the policy of "Nationalization"—a menace to our prosperity!—a threat to our Democracy!

BIBLIOLIFE

Old Books Deserve a New Life
www.bibliolife.com

Did you know that you can get most of our titles in our trademark **EasyScript**[TM] print format? **EasyScript**[TM] provides readers with a larger than average typeface, for a reading experience that's easier on the eyes.

Did you know that we have an ever-growing collection of books in many languages?

Order online:
www.bibliolife.com/store

Or to exclusively browse our **EasyScript**[TM] collection:
www.bibliogrande.com

At BiblioLife, we aim to make knowledge more accessible by making thousands of titles available to you – quickly and affordably.

Contact us:
BiblioLife
PO Box 21206
Charleston, SC 29413